The Sexual Mood

*

six short linked essays

*

Traumear

ii

*

Out of a consideration of what is defined as *a sexual mood* arise several other topics, developmentally, that are intended to add to our understanding of sex, gender, morality and ethics and finally of vicarious suffering.

*

Contents

*

The Sexual Mood

Is there anyone who can say in all good conscience – and awareness of self – he has never wronged the other sex? If he can, he will gain nothing from this present discourse because he will never have been in a sexual mood.

What I mean by this term is wrapped up with bad or guilty conscience vis-à-vis the other sex. I refer to male guilt before the female and female guilt before the male.

Usually when we feel guilt, we repress it. That's understandable. Guilt annoys, inconveniences and debilitates. It draws us into ourselves and makes us fearful. No wonder we negate it and generally pretend, as long as we can get away with it, that we are not guilty. We justify ourselves, in our own eyes and for the eyes of others. We judge so as not to be judged. We can become quite vehement. Some of our most flamboyant personality traits are out and out attempts to put guilt off our scent. Sexual guilt, incurred in the way we have behaved towards members of the other sex, is no different in this. Or we may be the types who, instead of protesting, decline. We go into decline before guilt. We hide. We hope that in the absence of any sign of ourselves the judge will overlook us. We would have to be hard pushed to be able to say who the judge is, but that makes no difference.

If we wish to come to grips with a guilty conscience, we must take care neither to self-assert nor to go into decline. The mood that accompanies guilt is the handle by which we can lift ourselves out of this sorry situation, this deplorable state. A sexual mood accompanies and introduces every instance of sexual guilt.

Describe this mood. It comes upon us like an accident – when we meet, or in the presence of, an agent of the other sex. I speak of an agent here because he or she must to some extent be sexually active; i.e. this individual must be consciously male or female but not conscientiously so, not masculine or feminine.

If I feel now that this should allow me to judge and condemn that individual, I am of course on the wrong track. To be conscious without being conscientious is certainly an incriminating state but condemnation makes matters worse, so that in addition I would incriminate myself. This may be a hard pill to swallow but all condemnation has that effect.

My first move, in the case of a sexual mood, must therefore be away from that sexually active individual and more effectively towards myself as someone in a sorrowful situation and in a deplorable state.

This move renders me conscientious and therefore right away gives me an edge over the unconscientious individual. By edge I mean a greater power of freedom.

*

Let me recapitulate. The sexual mood and the sexual guilt are inextricably linked. They are the same thing, viewed either morally or ethically. The moral point of view is limited to the realm of justice. It implies judgment, condemnation and punishment. That in itself is alright but how far does it actually get us, nowadays, if we really want to get ahead rather than getting tied up in

2

knots? Morality concentrates on what we 'get'. The ethic point of view entails all that – and goes beyond, making it possible for us to be effective and productive, not only individually but communally. (Generally we may think of ethics as communal growth and action including, or at least not excluding, morality.)

In that sense then, when we compare sexual guilt with a sexual mood, although we may suppose that we might gain by allocating blame correctly, in the case of guilt, and identifying causes for the purpose of future improvement, we soon discover that if our ambition is a permanent change to the good and not just a temporary change of appearances to the good, we can in fact come to grips with sexual moods, in ourselves, and make real headway.

First we need to spot them, to identify them and to admit to ourselves that this is indeed what they are. We mentioned earlier that in the semi-conscious presence of guilt we tend to cover it up or to hide from it, unaware that we make things worse like this. But leave that moral aspect of it to one side for the moment. Let's look at it ethically. A sexual mood is accompanied by pleasure, specifically by little pleasure, and by duplicity. So what happens, if we are not careful, is that we allow that little pleasure to divert our gaze from the duplicity, which then affects us destructively in the dark.

Assume for the moment that the sexual mood we mean here is a fact of experience for you at a certain time. You cannot go back on it, here it is, no use pretending that things are otherwise. Do you want to delude yourself now or do you want to behave with conse-

3

quence? Do you want to go for that little pleasure, maybe even stimulate and intensify it and turn it into a glorious myth, or do you intend to face up to the duplicity, which is not just a feeling of sorts but already a case of reprehensible behaviour.`

Confront the duplicity as behaviour, for which you can still be responsible, and you have a chance of progressing; but act out the pleasure and you lose track of the duplicity, mistaking its disappearance for non-existence. Or put it this way: As soon as you begin to act out the pleasure, the duplicity no longer exists but it *in*sists. It becomes the unconscious and destructive motor that drives your pleasure, and you into a tight corner.

The question is now: How can we respond maturely, with integrity, to our own duplicity, while we are still aware of it and not yet self-deluded by pleasure?

If we face our situation squarely – and conscientiously – we cannot help but be ashamed of ourselves. This shame is a direct outcome of our conscientious response to our discovery of duplicity on our part.

Once again forces come into play to make us, if at all possible, disown this shame. We can go off the track so badly that we say: If I feel shame I must have done something wrong, and since the conscientious response triggered off the shame, let me condemn and negate this conscientiousness. – We may stray quite far from recognizing the absurdity of this.

No, the useful thing is to let shame do its work. 'Are you not ashamed of yourself?' we say to a child who has misbehaved. In other words: 'Have you not brought your conscience into play?' It's one thing demanding it from a child, another to do it ourselves.

We can actually be ashamed.

Once we notice that we *happen* to be ashamed, due naturally to a conscientious move, we can then, in the interest of progress, actually decide to be ashamed.

The language to describe shame adequately seems a little remote nowadays. On occasions when we do respond conscientiously to some shortcoming in ourselves, we are perhaps more likely to try to take the rod of correction into our own hands, hoping to improve ourselves by an act of will, little realizing that of course our will itself is infected by the very malady we would like to cure. We pre-empt the feared punishment and forfeit the merciful strength.

When we notice that we have fallen into shame, we can decide to be ashamed, intentionally. We say yes to the shame although we know we are at liberty to say no to it, to mask it, to be ashamed of being ashamed.

Truly ethical behaviour involves merciful love. As soon as we say yes to the shame coincident with our conscientious response to our duplicity, we understand merciful love to the extent that is needful for us at that moment. We understand it in the sense that we subject ourselves to its healing influence and to its empowering effect.

To heal us of impotence and to endow us with power, this is the merciful love we mean in effect. Strength is the thing we lose when we indulge a sexual mood. But this is only the apparent strength, such as we mistakenly hoped to gain by going in for little pleasure, by sidestepping conscience and by disparaging shame. Such mortal strength is without foundation. Best let it be. Concentrate instead on gaining immortal strength, which cannot be destroyed or taken away.

We do well to cherish our mortality, our liability to dying, for by way of this same vulnerability arrives the eternal life for which we may provide.

* * *

The War of the Sexes

We stand in great need to be reminded of our mortality, especially while we live in an age when people are proud of their achievements and satisfied with their progress. At such times any philosophy or ethical system that holds out the desirability, and tempts us with the possibility, of an overall and automatic impunity and invulnerability, is especially dangerous because we are in effect made to feel obliged to lock the gate through which real life enters. The fact that real life cannot enter our being painlessly does not argue against the possibility of our preparing for it and so minimizing that pain and in any case rendering it, both in general and in the particular, significant.

One built-in guarantee against enduring presumption of immortality is the distinction of sex. We are born either male or female and there is no getting round that. There is however a way of getting round the tension and stress preternaturally inflicted by male upon female and by female upon male. We need to be careful how we understand this. We can kill pain and put off the day of reckoning. Instead we may suffer pain and hasten the day of mercy. Many times every day we may do one or the other, as we suppose we can, as we see fit or as we decide and choose.

In order to be able to decide judiciously or choose wisely on as many occasions as possible when it comes to such particularly sexual reminders of our mortality, we need to apprise ourselves of at least some of the ways in which the distinction of our sex renders us mortally vulnerable. This varies, of course, from one individual person to the next but certain common attributes become evident in response to enlightenment and insight.

To be male means to be nothing in itself except in relation to the female. Similarly, to be female means to be nothing in itself except in relation to the male.

This is a loaded statement, fraught with pitfalls and high potential. Be careful not to rush into any blatant agreement or disagreement. A relativist approach to sex definition would be as futile as an absolutist one would be bad. We need to look at sex, at the whole business of being created male or female, in the light of human maturation and ethical action.

When we ask: What does it mean to be male rather than female, or female rather than male, we are perhaps looking for some definition derived from maleness or femaleness itself, more specifically from male or female creatures themselves. We can come to a conclusion like this about a crab, say, or about a pine tree. We take a specimen aside, turn it this way and that way, observe it in action, relate to it in terms of use and so on. But there is no such thing in reality as a male or as a female. Not in the case of human beings, that is. An animal can be a male or a female, but a human being is male or female.

What are we to gather from this?

That which makes a human being observably male, and male in such a way that it makes sense to talk about it, comes into being not as a sex reflex but is brought into being generically and ethically.

The sex reflex is not something we do but it happens. We cannot even observe it happening, so it has always occurred, in the past, and then we may or may not take things from there. The sexual mood we discussed in the previous essay is evidence of a sex reflex in the past, no matter how long ago. Such a sexual mood is the same for a male as for a female human being. We cannot find out anything from it as to what it means to be male rather than female, or female rather than male. It is a reminder of our mortality. Such reminders are forceful in proportion to our presumption of immortality. We need to esteem them as a mercy, such reminders, because where immortality is not rooted in us and gained due to an overcoming of death, in other words where we have come into it presumptuously, or better: where we have come into a semblance of it presumptuously, there we need to be withdrawn and retrieved, or redeemed if you like, otherwise how can we have another chance, at the real thing?

So right from the outset, let us not in any way denigrate or speak pejoratively of this sex reflex, even though it does not directly lead to our manhood or womanhood, and even though it would seem to tempt us to destruction such as when we indulge a sexual mood.

It stands to reason, by the way, that we cannot really say anything sensible about such indulgence except from the perspective of an achieved ethical and generic context. Once we are free, we are able to estimate correctly what seemed at one time an onerous prison sentence, or even a pleasure taken in imprisonment, but not until then.

*

So 1. a sex reflex is in the past, 2. it guarantees nothing about or towards our mature manhood and womanhood and 3., it is accessible to us as a sexual mood. These three aspects of the sex-reflex we need to keep in mind.

Our next essay we intend to call The Creation of Gender. There it will become obvious what we can do and how we can behave if we wish to grow towards man- and womanhood rather than getting stuck immaturely in our sexuality. In the present essay we intend to analyze some of the errors we make, some of the misconceptions we favour and some of the myths about sexuality to which we cling, so that manhood and womanhood forever seem to move beyond our grasp.

1. First we look at the sex reflex as a thing of the past. It can never amount to a contemporary experience. We cannot be aware of it as it occurs. It is the sort of thing that 'must have happened, because look at this sexual mood'. The sexual mood is a projection into the present. It lingers. We may as well acknowledge here and now that present time is itself such a projection of the past, which lingers for a time, – except of course that it is pointless for us to try to distinguish between time (past, present and future) and the occurrences that are in them-

selves temporary. Past, present and future are temporary and therefore all distinguishable from eternity, which pertains to responses in awareness such as we will describe as ethical and generic in our next essay.

It seems indeed as if sexuality and temporality were extractable from the same root here. During our childhood, if indeed we were so fortunate as to have one, time was not what it is after puberty. With the onset of puberty, whether we see puberty now as a biological state or as a stage in growth and development, not only do sex reflexes occur, prior to experience, and do sexual moods come into being for experience, but past and present time, and therefore also future time, become separate entities, all of which we undergo as tension and stress. During childhood, and for children whose childhood has not been too terribly marred or mortified, time present, past and future are not yet problematic and we refer to this as dreamlike. We could also call it massive. While those who bring up children attempt, of course, to surround the child parentally with as wholesome a reality of eternal experience as possible, nevertheless this separation of past and present, mainly, from each other is unavoidable for the same reason as sex reflexes are unavoidable. We would go so far as to suggest that the two inextricably go hand in hand.

2. Next we try to come to terms, in our understanding, with sex reflexion as something that is in itself neither bad nor good, but simply an occurrence that should perhaps be described as elemental. Far from explaining any sexual mood, it is rather a way of coming to terms with the sort of thing that must have happened, in view of

our experience of a sexual mood. The moods themselves, in many cases, are open to a thousand and one interpretations but when we look for a cause, all we can come up with is, perhaps, a spark that has leaped, or a birth of consciousness, or however one would like to put it. We choose here to speak of a sex reflex, in particular, because we want to highlight the fact that for the first time, or as though it were for the first time, a human being comes into contact with a force, and more specifically with force in himself or in herself. In fact for the first time 'himself' and 'herself' becomes a relevant and telling expression for that being. The occurrence, or rather factuality, of a force within can be a shock, an eye-opener, a novelty. Keep in mind this is a force, not strength or power. It may seem dangerous because, as a force, it confronts us with, or causes us to confront, our lack of power and strength. A mature woman or man knows that the power and strength of merciful love is greater than any force, but no young person can really vouch for that. If maturity implies a familiarity with creative strength and power, then first of all the need for this must be brought home to us. We will not try to become strong if we are not convinced of the need for the good of strength by our experience of forces that can annihilate us while we are powerless and feeble.

Now we can speak of this sex reflex as a past contact with an elemental force. Any sexual mood is motivated, or perhaps we should say energized, by this, or like this, and it takes its peculiar colouring from the nature of the individual human being involved. Every human being will react in a unique way, and by reaction I mean something unconscious or sub-conscious and certainly nothing conscientious.

So we have all come across this sex reflex, this elemental force, in ourselves in the past, and we can say without a doubt that it can happen only because a male human being has been in the vicinity of a female human being, in which case either the one, or the other, or both will have reacted. (I realize, by the way, that I am expressing myself poorly at times here and my guess is that I have come up against major ignorance in myself.)

The reflex happened unconsciously and a result of it is a consciousness, in particular a consciousness of a sexual mood.

3. Now how can we come to terms with this mood? We have come up against an elemental force and the unconscious reaction which we called the sex reflex has certainly set us back into our male or female individuality. It has 'coloured' our individuality male or female. There is a first time for that. We are now, momentarily, consciously male or female individual beings. Conscientious we are not yet. If we are actually doing anything, it will probably be a forceful reaction, a conscious reaction against the force we have instinctively felt. Remember, we are nowhere near yet conscientiously effective in any way. The elemental force that has inwardly touched us has perhaps elicited from us a forceful reaction, or at least we have reacted forcefully, whether our reaction was elicited or not. Now this conscious reaction is not only peculiar in that it is male but also in that it posits a female object against which we pit ourselves. Or it is peculiarly female and posits a male object or thing against

which we pit ourselves, depending on whether we are female or male.

We have consciousness, male or female individuality and an involvement in a force field.

What I mean by a force field is a context of behaviour not in terms of love but of force.

What matters now is whether or not we are capable of conscience. If we are, and we choose to be conscientious, then this elemental force in which we have become involved becomes organic. If we are capable of conscience but do <u>not</u> choose to be conscientious then this force field in which we are involved becomes a turmoil and a dread for us and we are worried and harried, looking for enemies where there are none, mistaking actual friends and enemies, and unable to make friends. We are in a seriously problematic and complicated situation and in an unreal sense worse off than the one who is not capable of conscience, or less capable than ourselves, and this is of course because what conscience we <u>would</u> be capable of is working against us and condemning us.

In a real sense however we are better off than the one incapable of conscience, because all we have to do to escape from our predicament is become conscientious.

Now the one who is not capable of conscience, either because he has not been exposed to sufficient examples of it or because he has rejected them all, is in bad shape indeed, because he does not become organic but mechanic. His consciousness allows him to measure force against force, to pit energy against energy, and of course male against female. We may accurately refer to him as a male. A female being in such a predicament could then be called a female. (Remember that a human being cannot be a male of a female.)

The war of the sexes is always between males and females, and conscience does not play a role, only consciousness and force.

This lets us know why it is so crucially important that boys and girls are educated conscientiously, and are exposed to parental conscience in action and passion, to conscience in joy and suffering, so that when puberty sets in, they not only have the capacity for conscience but are likely to be conscientious, so that their adulthood will be mature and not immature.

* * *

The Creation of Gender

That which makes a human being observably male or female comes into being not as a sex reflex but generically and ethically. This we set down in our previous essay.

What we mean here is really an event, both generic and ethic. Not a reflex but a response is the beginning of it. In fact we must speak of responsible behaviour under certain conditions, and these conditions must be such that a choice could be made in the direction of our mortality, our liability to dying.

Nothing has happened in the past here, such as a sex reflex. Something goes on here and now, and two individual human beings are involved. Certainly one of them must be potentially masculine and the other potentially feminine, but prior to the event in question any maleness

14

and femaleness is a matter of appearances and not observable. Suddenly one notices that something is going on of a generic nature and even while it continues one may be a witness to it. What has triggered this event off? What has caused masculinity or femininity to come about? Nothing as such. All one can say is that the condition for it must have been right, while one cannot say why it came about at that particular time, or on that instance. Time in fact does not play a role in terms of past, present and future and there is no separation into tenses as in the case of a sex reflex.

How was the condition right for the apparent maleness to become actual masculinity, or for the apparent femaleness to become femininity? Why was there no sex-reflex but instead a generic response? Was the response conscious? Of course, responses are always at least conscious. A response to what?

Conscience must exist to some degree at least as a habit; in other words it must be unnecessary for conscience to be brought intentionally into play. There must be available a habit of conscience, due to a sufficient number of conscientious decision in the past. This habit of conscience is the ethic part of the condition, of the precondition, for the event of gender, or rather let us say for the event we are describing.

But then what about the fact that it is actually a response that is required and that a mere reaction or a reflex are out of order? Certainly a reflex or a reaction cannot be conscientious and we have already pointed to the prerequisite of conscience. At the same time we cannot point to anything prior to the generic event, such as to a sex reflex, because everything about this event is here and now.

Let us recall for the moment that masculinity and femininity occur simultaneously during a generic event. Certainly the male human being can respond ethically when confronted by a female individual who indulges meanwhile in a sexual mood but there will be no increase in masculinity for him, only in strength of character – which is no small thing of course. Similarly if a female human being is confronted by a male, who by definition is not conscientious, being a male individual by insisting on his apparent maleness, she will gain in strength of character by responding conscientiously but she will not become more feminine and more of a woman.

So the generic event requires the conscientious participation of both boy and girl. We might as readily say 'man and woman' except that we commonly do not employ those terms until a certain level of masculinity and femininity have been achieved. The terms young man and young woman might be taken to cover the transition period.

It becomes clear now that the other ingredient, in addition to conscience, is strength. Conscience makes for the ethical ingredient while strength makes for the generic.

And the same thing goes for strength as for conscience, that a habit of it must to some degree exist if the generic event is to come off and if masculinity and femininity are to come into being.

So an education that concentrates specifically on mature manhood and womanhood as its result will take care to inculcate above all strength and conscience.

However the strength and conscience we mean here are fundamental, not popular and social. And conscience is the more important. Where conscience exists, a sexual mood can be sustained and detached so that strength of character can increase, thus making it more likely that a generic event will occur in the fullness of time. Keep in mind that every generic event is spontaneous and that it cannot be manipulated or engineered into being. It is therefore also observably graceful.

*

Strength of character and conscience may both be inculcated or instilled in a child during his upbringing. The question is, how can one prepare a child for sexual moods and for generic events? As an adult I need only to keep on the look-out for sexual moods so that I will right away counter them conscientiously and strongly. Generic events I merely observe. But a child will experience a sexual mood and not know what to do with it.

It is the onset of puberty, which is on one hand a readiness to procreate the human species and on the other hand a readiness for masculinity and manhood, for femininity and womanhood.

The mortal aspect of this we have introduced in our previous essay. Reminders of our liability to die are sex reflexes and sexual moods, which signal the onset of puberty and leave us with a sense of liberty.

This sense of liberty, coincident with every intimation of mortality, we have not mentioned yet. We do not call it a facility of freedom but only a sense of liberty.

This sense of liberty may successfully be described to a young person ahead of time. There are many occurrences of it during youth, as childhood draws to a close and manhood or womanhood beckon. And on every occasion of such a sense of liberty, which the young person may be trained to detect, that same young person may decide – for death or for life.

Remember, if there were no mortality, or if the child had been trained to disabuse himself of his mortality, which might happen out of spiritualism, or if his mortality had never been drawn to his attention due to materialism, sex-reflexes would hardly be able to show up as sexual moods and would not be recognizable as such but would be masked by a myriad prejudices and superstitions, coloured politically, psychically, moralistically, etc., and then of course that crucial sense of liberty is adulterated and not detectable in distinction from those prejudices and superstitions, which are pursued or harboured dogmatically and licentiously.

A large responsibility rests with parental adults to acquaint children and young persons with their liability to die. Naturally only those mature persons who themselves are acquainted with eternal life, or real life, are able to do this. Of course it may be done more or less well.

Then the parental adult (parent, teacher, grandparent, uncle, etc.) watches out for those instances of liberty which open for the child like windows onto the world, or which is experienced like wings in readiness for flight. The adult does well to draw this to the attention of the young person, because here begins the great pedagogic task in terms of ethics and morality. The young person's behaviour during moments of liberty is decisive. Guidance is necessary. At the same time the youth becomes aware of moral choice and ethic selection.

We do well to handle these two in distinction. For the time being let us distinguish only along the following lines:

Moral choice reflects on advantages and disadvantages to myself as a sentient being.

Ethic selection entails the advantages equally to myself as a sapient being and to my community.

*

When a young person experiences a sense of liberty, this is the perfect time for an acquaintance with moral conscience and ethic strength. Whatever it is that happens during the onset of puberty – and we can describe it in a variety of ways – it leaves the young person for a moment at liberty and with a sense of that liberty. The youth is at liberty, but also at risk. Now it becomes apparent how he or she has been brought up.

This is in fact what it means, to be brought up or raised, namely to be made ready in terms of strength and conscience for the onset of puberty and therefore, by inference, for that sense of liberty which is not yet by any means a perception of freedom. Let us imagine a total lack of upbringing. In that case the sense of liberty is immediately mistaken for freedom so that action and behaviour must be at variance. The child is still in his natural dream state while the adult in total immaturity knows only appearances, mere appearances, so that the individual, unconscious child and merely apparent adult at once, will either behave like the blandest of philistines, holding the conventions sacred and legalistic with a vengeance, or else act the ignorant rebel, espousing revolution and anarchy, overthrowing limitations for no other reason than that they are limitations. The individual is torn, between childishness and adultery, between innocence and immaturity. The child has not been brought up, is unacquainted with conscience and strength and therefore cannot cope with the forces and laxities that beset him at the onset of puberty. The individual is in a pitiable state indeed. Of course he longs for freedom, but all he knows is reaction against forces, rebellion against constraints, indulgence in laxities and obedience to dogma. An insecure Society reveres the status quo and therefore finds fault only with the rebellious side of the unraised individual while sanctioning those individuals who feebly adhere to the dogma of the times. As soon as Society becomes arrogant, those who are feeble and young are sacrificed and the side of the un-brought-up individual which cannot bear constraint is given licence, so that Society, or the Nation, instead of decaying, may rush to its doom.

The son of man must be raised.

Now let us imagine someone who has been well brought up. Here the child has been gradually urged and wooed into wakefulness in loving anticipation of mature manhood or womanhood. Parental adults such as parents, relations and caring members of the community in the vicinity of the child, have conscientiously and by strength of personal example managed to acquaint the child with the true benefits and real advantages of morality and ethics, of conscience and strength, with the desirability of responsible freedom. Now, at the onset of puberty, when the son of man 'comes like a thief', the young person will experience that sense of liberty not superstitiously or presumptuously but as a harbinger of freedom so that right away or soon enough the steps of moral behaviour and ethical action are taken, from this liberty in the direction of freedom. Only then can the son of man eventually be seen 'coming in power with the clouds of heaven'.

Sex is a business of males and females, while gender is to do with men and women.

Once we have experienced in ourselves the wonder of gender we avoid the vexations of sex. Any sexual mood, whether original in us or transferred to us, we confront with conscientious strength, thereby adding to our preparedness for generic events.

But all creation is twofold. Not only can we get conditions ready, prerequisite for the event, but we can also transmute whatever seems to stand in the way or in any way seems to hinder either progress towards manhood or womanhood or the advent of it, its arrival, in our being. A mature human being, morally sound and ethically complete, appreciates the continuous arrival, on the doorstep of his experience, of that which sustains him in life and at the same time allows him to sustain others, such as those who are not yet mature or indeed immature. A generically perfect person, in other words a true man or woman, stands firmly in the mainstream of human creativity and growth, and whenever something seems to impede the free flow of dynamic life, into him and from him, he cheerfully suffers that hindrance, by taking the responsibility for it and for an increased willingness to change.

We do well therefore to think of gender as something that becomes personally relevant to us at puberty when a tremendous process of learning begins which culminates in our mature appreciation of eternal life on earth as we work and grow.

The conscientious and strong response to sexual moods is certainly an achievement, and all such achievements prepare the ground for eventual gender. We refer to such achievements as masculinity and femininity. (Females are not feminine, males are not masculine.) But the generic event, and thereafter any generic event, is spontaneous and carefully observed. Gratitude, generosity and magnanimity all play into it.

Due to our observation of what goes on and comes about during any generic event we become more and more involved in it and involved with it, so that that which was at first an unfamiliar and perhaps startling experience gradually turns into habits of action and patterns of behaviour, that are not only masculine but manly and not only feminine but womanly. As mature human beings, we are either men or women, so that our humanity and our gender are in the end one. (In the case of sexuality, humanity is at variance with itself.)

The creation of our manhood and womanhood entails an exacting process of observation of those particular phenomena that have to do with our pride and our sense of justice. One of the most difficult operations of the human intellect, of human intellection, is the discernment of moral motivations as distinct from ethical considerations. In our next essay we try to make this distinction.

*

Moral and Ethical in Relation to Gender

As a sentient being, as someone who can sense this and that and who can have a sense of this and that, I am able to reflect on the advantages and disadvantages that accrue to me in accordance with moral choices I make.

Now I call it a moral choice if I am not so much guided in my behaviour by pleasure and pain, by convenience and inconvenience, comfort and discomfort, but by what I believe or assume is better and more worthwhile than this.

In relation to my being male (not a male) this means that I reflect on the benefits, to myself, of bringing children into the world, (or conversely on the benefits to myself of not bringing them into the world), as of greater importance and as worthy of a higher consideration than sexual sensuality or even sensuous sexuality.

This is not the same as saying that having children is more important than having sex. It may, for example, be due entirely to moral reflection that I decide not to have children even though my sexuality urges me to sexual intercourse with the other sex. Conversely I may decide I want to have children even though sexual intercourse is painful, inconvenient or uncomfortable for me.

It is a characteristic in general of what we mean by morality, that reflection plays a role and that however else I may choose to present my case, the good of it has to do with myself and not at all with anyone else. I may reflect on such a thing as moral causes, for instance, as on charitable causes, on altruistic or philanthropic impulses or purposes, but all the time I have in mind what this means to me as a sentient being, as someone who prefers to see himself in this light or that light, or who prefers to be seen by those around him in one way or another.

Now morality naturally leads into ethics. We can never make a successful argument for moral action alone, or for merely moral action, such as when we try to stop with reflections on what does us good as long as it hurts no one else.

Not that our moral advantage is bound by necessity to imply someone else's disadvantage, this is not the crux of the matter. It is quite possible to do moral good without harming anyone – as long as by harm we mean, again, moral harm.

However – and this is the crucial thing – were we to insist on moral reflection, and on morality, and on moral choices as our highest and greatest possible good, rather than, perhaps, our greatest approach to it, we would hamper the ethos of our human being, which exists in communality.

This is the only way in which morality might get in the way of our best interests, loosely speaking. As the approach to ethical considerations, morality cannot go wrong. But any moral attempt to grasp the good is not only futile from the start but, pursued as policy, social or cultural, it spells ruin for communication and community.

And any personal insistence on moral superiority only isolates the individual and renders him ineffective, even in the midst of the most popular acclaim.

*

Gender is not primarily to do with the procreation of the human species but with our manhood and womanhood. It might be a good idea to emphasize now and again that we long for mature human being alright but that we cannot be mature unless we are mature women and mature men. Reflections on moral advantage and disadvantage pertain to human beings as such and no adjustment is required to allow for gender. As soon as we become concerned with our ethos however, male and female gender come into their own, so that manhood and womanhood must be considered in distinction.

It stands to reason therefore that morality itself needs to be viewed from an ethical point of view, just as sexuality needs to be understood from the point of view of gender. Our understanding, in other words, must begin at the point of ethos and gender if we are to learn anything sensible about morality and sex.

We intend, here, to make use of the distinction between choice and selection, specifically in the way we speak of moral choice and ethic selection.

A prerequisite for ethic selection is a perception of the good. By the good we mean that which is good in itself and good quite independently of whether we perceive it or not. Let us ignore, for the moment, that cleansing and hygiene are prerequisites for any perception of the good and ask directly, in the company of those who are sufficiently clean: How do we select in accordance with what is truly and independently good? How can we tell that something will be of advantage equally to ourselves and to those in our community? Obviously a kind of special wisdom is required. In the previous essay we distinguished between sentient and sapient. To be sentient means to have a sense of this or that, but to be sapient, as we intend to use the word here, means to have perception, or to be perceptive, not of this or that, but of the good. Not morality, but ethics entails such perception.

Selection, in the light of this, does not involve comparison, as does choice. When I choose, I compare this to that first. I also evaluate. This is better than that, so I choose it. Comparison involves a standard. This is better than that in terms of a third thing. We speak, therefore, of such a thing as a moral standard. But when we select, we know that our selection will be good, not better or best.

Also, and perhaps most important, we select because we intend to act. We know that whatever we select will be good because our action, which implies the selection, involves both us and our selection in a good work. The fact that I myself am bound to be implicated due to any ethic selection on my part is the crucial factor. This is why so little actual ethic selection takes place, because we want to remain untouched and ''untainted' by our – moral choices. All ethical behaviour involves our contact with the good, and this contact is fruitful if we are 'clean' but painful to the extent that we are not clean. An ethically committed person welcomes this pain because it points the way for further cleansing and ultimate fruitfulness. Any morally exclusive – or exclusively moral – individual however senses the pain and immediately shies away from the ethic challenge. Such an individual prefers seeming morally superior to people to being fruitful and doing good, which often is accompanied by mere appearances of failure.

So we can say that the moral individual either gets ready for ethical action or becomes moralistic. Morality itself is mistakenly rejected by many because they see only the bad examples of those who have become moralistic. At the same time of course it cannot be ignored that their rejection of morality is itself a moralistic move, and a sign of their unwillingness to be touched by the good.

We all of us have within us at least a drive, if not a more or less conscious desire, for manhood or womanhood. We can also describe this as the need to mature. Human maturity is inseparable from manhood and womanhood.

Now our wish for community goes hand in hand with this. Maturity, community, manhood and womanhood, all these must be seen as originating within and among us. They are not, creatively, and cannot be, successfully, imposed from outside.

Any worthwhile notion that you or I have of what it means to be a communal human being stems from our perception of the good and from our being, or having been, ethically moved or touched by the good. Society has to do with moral standards. Community is by definition ethic.

When we contemplate the meaning of community in this light, we can see that it pertains to a few, to several and to many, but never to all. The concept of community implies a gradation of involvement. This personal involvement and commitment is essential as soon as we speak of *a* community, because then we must mean at the same time mine or yours or someone else's. Members of my community may be (however need not be) relations by blood, friends and companions, acquaintances, neighbours, the milkman and others in my vicinity with whom I have only a casual contact, and in addition to this all those whose books and compositions and paintings matter to me, because through their works I know them too and they make a difference to me even if I may not any longer be able to make one to them.

When we say that you and I belong to the same community, then this can only mean 'approximately the same', because you are bound to have acquaintances other than mine, and even if we both knew exactly the same number of human beings only, as one might picture happening on a small island, then the nature and quality of our various personal connections and contacts would still be different.

A communal human being is therefore one who is aware, on one hand, of personal contact in the way above described, but on the other hand the overriding nature or essence of this connection must be a renewing love.

The difference between society and community must therefore be looked at. What we see when we study social structures is not an expression of renewing love at all but repeated attempts at compromise solutions of survival problems, and when we take a close look at what travels under the banner of personality, of personal contact and connection, we notice how time and again personality is in fact sacrificed to those compromises and in any case given second place, depending on survival.

If mature manhood and womanhood in community are to be more than empty words or hypocritical stances for us, then they must be our chief considerations, and only then will we understand the true meaning even of survival. Only from the point of view of a renewing communal love do we gain insight into the dependent character of all survival issues in relation to live communality and personhood.

Those who have been touched by the good, thirst and hunger for truth, while those who have not been touched by the good are bound to wonder: What is this, the good? For them there is no such thing as 'the good', and they cannot conceive of truth as anything other than what is right and correct and just. Also the very notion of renewing love will seem superfluous to them. At the same time those with knowledge and experience of the good, either from birth of thereafter, are bound to make use of this 'sapience' or wisdom and to exemplify it. They are not so much concerned with any liberty to make moral choices but with the freedom to be ethically selective. Such ethical selection is not according to standards but from that wisdom which grows out of their inward and outward acquaintance with the good. (Moral choices pertain to us as liberated sentient beings. Ethic selection is possible for us as free sapient beings. Many are capable of sensation but not of wisdom, but those few who have the wisdom have also the sense.)

29

It remains for us now to acknowledge that true human maturity comes along with ethical selection. If I have the wisdom for ethical selection (the sapience) and if I then do work in line with this, being ethically selective and selecting ethically, then my maturity is assured – and I am a man or a woman.

Ethic selection is really a response to the good. Once we are free we are grateful for that freedom and once we have life we want to continue to give that life. So we look for opportunities to express our gratitude. This may prove difficult enough if we are surrounded by those whose morality does not extend into an ethical frame of reference and so the life we wish to give is not readily accepted. We may end up being more than doing. We can be examples but when it comes to doing good the illusion of survival gets in the way of our being understood. Society collapses and community is not espoused. Morality becomes exclusive and ethics no longer has any appeal. It turns out time and again that we must wait and that the way we wait makes a difference. For our own sake we can reach out into the realm of the good and make a thousand discoveries, but when it comes to sharing these, we are forced to confess our ineptitude and declare ourselves impotent. The best we can do is offer.

A little effort is required to take us over that familiar hump of resentful indifference. This small step in the right direction is our active wish to live in spite of our seeming inability to share our life. We do not even need to feel ourselves making this small effort; the wish to make it suffices.

What happens then guarantees us our maturity as men and women within an ethical community while those who insist on morality as final shun us.

* * *

Moral Motivation – Ethical Consideration

A small effort in response to the good is the beginning of all ethical action. However the response must be to the good and not to some idea of the good. Therefore the good must be held in trust. To a sentient being this makes no sense. Ideas are required before a thing can be imagined. But the good is no thing and an idea of it precludes ethical responsibility. The sentient being therefore can at best come up with a half-way ethic as an extension of a survival morality.

The good we hold in trust is personal. It is the priceless pearl. The sentient being would tend to picture it but it must be hidden. Therefore we make sure to believe in it. Only in that way does the good retain its potency for us.

Loosely speaking we can believe in whatever we like and draw the consequences. But just as there is a proper way of walking, by placing one foot in front of the other, though we can shuffle sideways if we like, so there is also a proper way of believing, and that is in the good we hold hidden in trust. Our believing must be rooted in the good, only then will we profit and benefit from believing what we believe. So if I believe that you mean to harm me, this is something useful for me to do only if my believing is done in the good.

We have to be very careful with our language because the halfway ethic of sentient being overlies with its traditions and conventions the truth we need to know and wish to state.

So, if we believe *in* something, this is not the same as believing it. Whatever I believe, I believe to be true. Of course the truth extends into the world of phenomena, so that I may believe that a particular door is closed when in fact it has meanwhile been opened. But the point is, that even in such a case it does me good, it is of advantage to me, to believe that it is closed, if I do my believing in the good I secretly hold in trust. From the point of view of sentience this must seem absurd but that is because from such a point of view believing is synonymous with assuming and supposing, and certainty can be gained only according to appearances, at best sensible appearances. To the one who holds the good in trust, this is foolishness and he may try to persuade the sentient being to be sapient and to believe in the good and to build his certainty on the truth rather than on appearances, but finally it all depends on whether that being is first touched by the good.

Whatever we believe, then, if we do not believe it in the good, it does us no good to believe it.

*

The halfway ethic of sentient beings is really a false extension of morality into the ethical realm. It comprises something like making moral choices on behalf of others. It would therefore be quite inappropriate to suppose that pushing such a halfway ethic to the extreme could amount to anything useful. What is required instead is a retractions. The victim of his own ego must return to his as yet unethical morality and examine it in terms of the good he has begun to believe in, having been touched by the good. He will now come to recognize that every small effort he makes in response to that hidden good causes his morality, coincidentally, to become once again sympathetic and generous, in anticipation of the eventual truly ethical compassion and mercy.

The small effort we make in response to the good entails a direction of our entire sentient being. We may be accustomed to making huge sensational efforts, so what we do now tends to seem ineffectual. Time and again we will have to gear ourselves down to that small effort, but in response to the good; it takes time to replace bad habits with good ones.

It helps if we insist that our small effort of a response be grateful and cheerful, because this helps us keep in mind that the response is personal, not to a thing, and that it automatically overcomes any hindrance. In gratitude to the good, then, we respond to it, and remain evidently unimpressed by anything that would seem to make our response difficult or even impossible. In truth it is easy.

*

Eventually then we will once again recognize a moral motivation as something that springs from our sound human being, and in such a way that we do not first have to calculate comparative advantages but we will know from the outset, intuitively, that certain claims being made on us, of duty or obligation, leave us free to respond ethically. Formerly we wrongly imagined that whatever occurred to us within a moral context had to be dealt with in that same context or else we left ourselves open to obloquy. No wonder that with the best of conscientious wills we always felt we fell short somehow, either because our ideals were perhaps not fully formed or on account of insufficient effort. Nor does the traditional controversy of faith versus action add anything useful, because after all justification is still the goal, and justification makes sense only in a moral context. Any attempt to inflate this context so that it might eventually do duty as a vehicle sufficient towards human freedom ends by placing burdens on others, dogmatically, and by a resignation to a secret futility in ourselves.

Ethical considerations are such that the good plays a role and has a say in them. The personal good is therefore a part of our ethical consideration. It becomes a point of honour, of honourable pride for us, that no moral motivation pertinent to us is left without its ethical consideration. Every appeal that is made to us in terms of morality, of what we owe to ourselves and to others, is immediately transubstantiated by us as we begin by making a small effort in response to the good. In that way we acknowledge most effectively that even the moral motivation is a good challenge. Beyond that we create an ethical context, by our small effort in response to the personal good, within which all moral problems are solved and moral tensions dissolved.

When we are active strictly from moral motivation we ask ourselves only how we can best achieve whatever goal we have accepted as ours. The morality of hard work and just reward is familiar to us all. So is the related notion of self-sacrifice. The thinking here is that by willingly destroying our self in the service of something we take to be greater than ourselves we actually manage to do the good which we deeply within ourselves want to do. The desire to do good is so fundamental and original in us that we do not readily perceive it as such. But whether we are born in the lap of the good or touched by it later in life, or both, what matters for our eventual happiness and satisfaction, our 'blessedness', is that the good we do somehow measures up to the good we inherited and experienced. Hence the saying: The more that is given to us, the more is expected.

Moral motivation is a start, and we do well to understand it as a kind of beginner's encouragement to do good. Children are morally motivated within their community and their parental elders then gradually bring the maturing child around to ethical consideration. There is the danger on one hand of morality growing cold as its insufficiency vis-à-vis the deep desire to do good becomes evident and on the other hand of morality being strained, as we mentioned elsewhere, and of being asked to cover areas of experience for which it has no relevance, even to the point of fanaticism.

To be morally motivated means to have experienced an urge to do good and then having reflected on that urge, so that we say to ourselves: How can I go ahead now and do what I feel I ought to do? The moral motivation, in other words, is separate from the world of action, so that sometimes a great deal of cogitation is required before we make a choice or a decision. We weigh up the consequences of behaving one way or another. We wonder which would be the more meaningful course. Perhaps we allow ourselves to be guided by principles.

We may speak of a moral urge and of a moral compulsion. We may decide on a course of action as good even though others disagree with us. So our individuality may be at stake. Sometimes, for the sake of our individuality and so that it may remain intact, we occupy our minds with a great diversity of notions and ideas and we become like hunters for prize game, up all night and with no time for anything except this vehement search for that which will assure us of our humanity. A human being insecure as to his or her humanity can be in a desperate state. Is it not as if the world itself were being withheld from such a being, and all too often what happens is that an ambition arises to 'conquer the world', in other words to make all things out there answer somehow to our notions about them in here. So we manipulate appearances, and this is not good. We set out to change the world, and that is not good either. All that can help us is the good, for it is the good we do which assures us of our humanity and nothing else will do.

When we recognize that being human and doing good in our case is one and the same, we begin to see our morality in a different light. We recognize that morality alone cannot put us in touch with our humanity. Something additional is required. The urge to do good is upon us but morality eventually only feeds our illusion of *being* good. This can only ever be an illusion. Meanwhile our desire for exemplifying the good is not an illusion but real.

The breakthrough from morality to ethics can be quite epoch-making. We have engineered every one of our moves, we have predicted every eventuality and have left nothing untried. Those around us who observe our progress know what we want and do their best to keep us on course. They know there is one thing they cannot do for us, which is the same as what we cannot do for ourselves, and that is the gaining of a command over the personal good. Here we must measure up to requirements we can neither second-guess nor calculate. There is a teaching we can take to ourselves but once again we must be careful to distinguish between what we must do and what we cannot do, between what we should take great care not to neglect and what we should definitely ignore and forget.

When the personal good is shown to us, we will not be in any doubt about it. No longer are we in doubt about our humanity. We know now that something exists in the flesh and in reality which previously had only historic connotations and ideal characteristics. Our idea and report of the good and of the personal good is now replaced by experience of it in reality and in the world. Naturally everything is bound to change for us now. Previously we lived in the present, came out of the past and headed into the future. Of that we were conscious and we thought in those terms. Space had nothing to do with time except insofar as we imagined or dreamt it.

Now we discover to our surprise that space and time really amount to the same. We see no more reason why we should assume that the universe is finite.

Above all we are bound to acknowledge now that it has become possible for us to have input into our fate. We can 'do' in such a way that we overcome our present carnal limitations. Typically those limitations are modes of unhappiness. They are apparent constraints on our freedom, on our free being and behaviour.

The secret of course now is that when we do, we no longer collaborate with forces. Instead we rely on good strength. This strength must be considered as part and parcel of our ethical conscience. We do not apply it but we apply for it, even as we know what we do.

An application for strength is a part of every ethical act. It is in this way that whatever appears to stand between our desire to do good and the realization of that desire is overcome. What we cannot dictate however is the time. The strength we apply for is given immediately and does its work but we cannot say how long the work will take to come to fruition.

On that account alone, many who have experienced the effective strength for the personal good have slid back into morality alone, so that they might have the illusory good right away instead of the good reality in its own time.

True patience is for that reason highly prized. It allows us to wait for what in our wisdom we know to be in process though we have no sensation of it. Ethical behaviour is always truly patient. As we consider the various possibilities of change to the good, we do not reflect on them, knowing that we cannot because until they have been realized they have neither form nor shape for us. We are in the possession of a general outline of what we hope to achieve, but even this, as we know, might be changed suddenly, so we cling to no thing. We continue to consider all possibilities. There are no signs of progress because we ourselves are personally involved in it. All too often we become inconsiderate because we become attached momentarily to some sensation and right away we become involved in moral reflection. What is gone then is final and perfect rest, which accompanies all ethical consideration. Along with such restlessness comes moral justification, issues of righteousness, illusions of success and self-worth, and intimations of popularity.

This perfect rest then is the single thing that is necessary because we can hold on to it without clinging to it. Our mindfulness of it is a prudent move. Eventually we learn how to relax right into it, so that we are then most unlikely to be waylaid by moral reflections on what seems to move us.

* * *

Ethics and Suffering

Those who are capable of ethical being, behaviour and action do not suffer on their own behalf but for others.

Let us for a moment recall, that when the personal good has touched us we are finally whole. What is it now that we should do? Gloat and boast about it? What is the point of the good spirit becoming incarnate in any case? Certainly we are not to turn into a collection of perfect, isolated individuals. The community of men, women and children on earth is our goal, and it is the good spirit which sets us this goal, whether from birth or rebirth.

So how is it possible that those who are whole nonetheless are mortal and acquainted with pain? They cannot fall into morbid conditions of their own account. It is the presence of others that infects them with mortality and pain. Also they are affected by the condition of others.

The reason for this is obvious. If the blessedness they have gained is not to pass from them ineffectually then they must pass it on. They must, so to speak, become a blessing for those around them. How can they succeed in this except by taking upon themselves, gladly, the pain that comes their way and by suffering it cheerfully for those who have not yet been touched by the good?

We give to this the name of vicarious suffering.

The art that springs from vicarious suffering can itself be understood as vicarious, in terms of reality. Like all genuine art, it involves creativity for others, not for the self or for society, but in addition a work process is entailed where the art worker assumes in his person, as part of a fundamental stance, the pain of the members of his community.

First, of course, the art worker must be a member of a community and must see himself as tied by a bond of fidelity to a few, to several, or to many human beings. They must be human beings and not people. The bond of community does not coincide with, but cuts across all conventional boundaries of family, tribe, society, class, nation and so on. The community we mean does not exist by appointment but it gradually grows as every human being's ever changing circle of companions, acquaintances and friends, including personal contacts and relationships of every imaginable sort, and the common denominator, the link or cement, is human being.

The vicarious art worker assumes in his person the burden of pain of his community. He remains in touch, he communicates, with the members of his community. He sees himself as a caretaker. He is the exact opposite of a show-off who produces arbitrary or magical sensations for money or popular esteem.

* * * *